三か国語連詩
三国语言连诗
삼개국어 연시
TRILINGUAL
RENSHI

Acknowledgements: The authors would like to thank the following journals in Japan, China, and Korea which will publish this Trilingual Renshi in each respective language simultaneously in August 2015: 現代詩手帖 (*Gendaishi Techo* of Sichosha), Tokyo, Japan; 诗歌月刊 (*Poetry Monthly* of Anhui Province Arts & Literature Alliance), China; 월간 현대시 (*Monthly Contemporary Poetry*), Seoul, Korea.

The authors would also like to express their gratitude to LTI Korea (Literature Translation Institute of Korea) for its generous support. Thank you to Deborah Woodard, Sarah Ream, and Michele Hutchison for reading and giving us helpful editorial suggestions for the poems in English translation. And thank you, Mia You, the central web editor of Poetry International Rotterdam, in advance for featuring the Trilingual Renshi including the special video version (http://www.poetryinternationalweb.net). The publisher would like to offer special thanks to Mizuho Takahashi of MEM gallery and Natsumi Hayashi and Hisaji Hara for the cover image *Today's Levitation 01/01/2011*.

First published 2015 by Vagabond Press.

PO Box 958 Newtown NSW 2042 Australia
www.vagabondpress.net

Cover image: *Today's Levitation 01/01/2011* ©Natsumi Hayashi, courtesy MEM, Tokyo.
Designed and typeset by Michael Brennan in MS Mincho, SimSun, Batang and Book Antiqua 10.5/14.

ISBN 978-1-922181-44-2

三か国語連詩
三国语言连诗
삼개국어 연시
TRILINGUAL RENSHI

詩 POEMS
四元康祐 YASUHIRO YOTSUMOTO（日/Japanese）
明迪 MING DI（中/Chinese）
金惠順 KIM HYESOON（韓/Korean）
谷川俊太郎 SHUNTARŌ TANIKAWA（日/Japanese）

翻訳 TRANSLATIONS
YASUHIRO YOTSUMOTO (Japanese) MING DI (Chinese) DON MEE CHOI (Korean)

VAGABOND PRESS
ASIA PACIFIC POETRY 2015

CONTENTS

海の巻
海之卷
바다

THE ROLE OF 'SEA'

1

(康/Yasuhiro)

サンマルコ広場の波止場でスーツケースを引き摺る
三人の娘たち　黒い髪　黒い眼
どこから来たのかな？黙っていたなら
三羽の鴎みたいに区別がつかない
ねえ、声を聴かせて

三个女孩提着行李箱来到圣马尔谷广场
码头上，三个女孩黑发，黑眼睛
不知来自哪里
她们沉默，像三只海鸥，分不清谁是谁
嘿，让我们听一听你们的声音

검은 머리 검은 눈 세 소녀가
산 마르코 광장의 부두에서 가방을 끌고 가고 있다
이 소녀들은 어디에서 왔을까
서로를 분간하기 힘든 갈매기들처럼 아무 말도 없이
헤이, 너희들 목소리를 들려줘봐

Three girls with black hair and black eyes
carrying suitcases on the pier of Piazza San Marco.
I wonder where they come from? Silent, they are
like three seagulls, hard to tell one from the others.
Hey, let us hear your voices!

2

（迪／Mindy）

爱丽尔哼起一支曲，海风把声音传送
至咖啡馆，一位白发男子抬头
看见三姐妹，白杨树影在他眼中晃动

아리엘은 작게 노래 흥얼거리고 바다 바람은 노래의 선율을 나른다
카페에선 백발 노인이 그 세 자매를 바라보고 있는데
포플라나무 그림자가 그의 눈에 어린다

エリアルが口ずさんだ鼻歌を、海風がカフェへと
運んでゆく、すると白髪のおじいさんがふと顔をあげて
三人の姉妹を見つめる、その瞳に白樺の木の影が映っている

Ariel hums a little song, the sea wind carries her tune
to a cafe, where a white-haired man looks up
and sees the three sisters, poplar shadows in his eyes

3

（惠/Hyesoon）

갈매기도 잠든 깜깜한 밤
아이들이 슈트케이스를 끌고 떠나고 있다
모두 잠들었는데 아이들만 깨어 있다
서쪽 부두에서 아무도 몰래 배가 출항하고 있다
일 년 째 같은 아이들, 같은 배, 같은 구름, 같은 하늘이 떠나고 있다.

鴎も眠る、丑三つ時
子供たちは立ち去ってゆく、スーツケースをがらがら引いて
誰もかもが眠っている　子供たちのほかは
西向きの岸壁から、人知れずフェリーが出てゆく
この一年というもの、同じ子らの出発、同じフェリー、同じ雲、同じ空。

漆黑的夜晚，海鸥在睡眠
孩子们在离开，拖着行李箱
所有人都睡着了，除了孩子们
西边码头，轮渡悄悄离开。一年了
同一只船，孩子们离开，如同样的云，离开同样的天。

A pitch-dark night, even the seagulls are asleep
The children are leaving, dragging along their suitcases
Everyone's asleep except for the children
From the western pier, a ferry departs secretly
For a year, same departing children, same ferry, same clouds, same sky.

4

(俊/Shuntarō)

前世で乗っていたノアの方舟
今は海底で朽ち果てている
結局地球の外には出られなかったのだ

우리가 전생에 승선했던 노아의 방주는
이제 심해의 바닥에서 썩고 있다
결국, 지구 밖으로는 나갈 수 없다

前世乘过的诺亚方舟
此刻腐烂在海底
毕竟，它走不出地球

The Noah's Ark we boarded in our previous lives
now lies rotten on the ocean floor.
After all, it couldn't get out of the earth…

5

(康/Yasuhiro)

詩を書くたびに僕は月へ昇り
静かの底に座ってわが故郷を見下ろす
その冷たい青に秘められた血の赤に目を凝らして
海が僕らを互いから分け隔て
海が僕らを互いに結び付けている

每次写诗我都会爬到月亮上
坐在静谧深处，俯瞰我的家乡
试图看清那隐藏在冷蓝中，血一样的红色
同一个海连接我们
同一个海分离我们

나는 시를 쓸 때마다 달에 올라가
고요의 바닥에 앉아 우리 집을 내려다보면서
차가운 파랑에서 피의 붉음을 보려고 애쓰고 있다
바다는 우리를 서로 서로 나누어 놓지만
그 바다는 또 우리 서로 서로를 이어준다

Each time I write a poem I climb up to the moon, and sit
at the bottom of Tranquility, looking down on my home,
trying to see the red of blood hidden in that cold blue.
It's the sea that separates us from each other,
the same sea that connects us to each other.

6

(迪/Mindy)

今晚，天空是黯淡的船舱——
我们醒着，眼睛是一只只新月
驶向彼此共和的太阳

오늘밤 하늘은 깜깜한 선실이다——
우리는 깨어 있고, 우리의 눈동자 각각은 새로 뜨는 달이다
태양 공화국으로 노 저어가는

今宵、空は昏い船室——
私たちは目覚めている、それぞれに新月の眼を見開いて
太陽を共に和するために船出してゆく

Tonight the sky is a dark cabin—
we're awake, our eyes each a new moon
sailing to a Sun Republic

7

(惠/Hyesoon)

전깃줄 위 새들의 날개가 젖어 있다
열리지 않는 문을 긁어대던 손톱들처럼 벚꽃잎이 지고 있다
먼 산 위의 태양이 흠뻑 젖어 무거워지고 있다
바다로 만든 사람이 창문 밖에 서 있다
새벽 안개처럼 얇아 안을 수 없는 사람이다

電線に止まった小鳥たちの翼が濡れている
桜の花の散りゆくさまは開かずの扉を引っかく指爪のようだ
遠い山並みの上に、びしょびしょの太陽がのしかかる
窓の外には海で出来た誰かが佇んでいるけれど
その人を抱きしめることはできない、朝靄みたいにすかすかなので

鸟栖息在电线上，羽翼潮湿
樱花落下，像指甲抓打那打不开的门
远处山上，湿透的太阳沉重
一个水做的人站在窗外
无法支撑，枯瘦如早晨的雾

Perched on a power line, the birds' wings are wet
Cherry blossoms fall like fingernails scratching a door that won't open
Above the faraway mountain, the drenched sun becomes heavy
Someone made of ocean stands outside the window
That someone can't be held, so thin like the morning fog

8

(俊/Shuntarō)

プランクトンはどんなソフトでデザインされたのだろう
顕微鏡から目を離していっとき放心している少年は
神という言葉を使わずに世界を夢想したいのだ

什么样的软件设计出这些浮游生物？
小男孩纳闷了片刻，目光离开显微镜
他想不用"上帝"这个词来幻想世界

무슨 소프트웨어 앱이 플랑크톤을 디자인했을까
현미경에서 눈을 뗀 소년이 잠시 마음을 내려놓는다
소년은 '신'이란 단어를 쓰지 않고도 세상을 꿈 꾸고 싶다

What kind of software application designed plankton?
The boy lets his mind wander for a moment, his eyes away from the microscope.
He wants to dream about the world without using the word 'God'.

9

(迪/Mindy)

文字穿行——如影子。苹果高歌——
iPhone, iPad, iPod, iTunes——掀动海底。
飓风，海啸。然后是寂静，寂静。爱丽儿姐妹们
将语言藏于金色的珊瑚中。深水之上，
文字再次启程，如鱼群，穿行于有咸味的海浪与海草。

문자는 여행한다——그림자처럼, 애플은 노래한다——
iPhone, iPad, iPod, iTunes——바다를 휘저으며.
허리케인과 쓰나미, 그 다음 모두 정적, 정적. 아리엘의 자매들은
금빛 산호 속에서 그들의 말을 지켜냈다. 심해를 넘어,
문자들은 다시 여행한다, 물고기처럼, 소금바다와 해초를 넘어.

文字は旅する——影のように。林檎は歌う——
iPhone, iPad, iPod, iTunes——海原を振るわせながら。
台風そして津波。それからみんなしーんと静まりかえる。エリアル姉妹が
自分たちのお喋りを金の珊瑚に仕舞いこむ。深い水のなかでは、
ふたたび文字が旅に出る、魚のように、しょっぱい波と海藻を潜り抜けて。

Words travel—as shadows. Apples sing—
iPhone, iPad, iPod, iTunes—stir the oceans.
Hurricanes and tsunamis. Then all is quiet, quiet. Ariel sisters
guard their speeches in golden corals. Above the deep water,
words travel again, as fishes, over the salty waves and seaweed.

10

(康／Yasuhiro)

窓から見下ろす北斎の駿河湾
高度３万フィートで頬張る海苔巻き
あの人の頬伝う涙の味を思い出している心の雲……

眺望窗外，下面是北斎画过的骏河湾
三万米高处，满嘴海苔寿司
她心中的云铭记着面颊上滚落的泪水味道……

창문으로 호쿠사이의 스루가만을 내려다본다
3만 피트 높이에서 입안 가득 노리마끼를 입에 물고
그녀의 뺨위로 굴러떨어지던 눈물의 맛을 마음에 피는 구름으로 떠올리면서

Hokusai's Suruga Bay gazed upon through the window.
Mouthful of *Norimaki* at an altitude of 30,000 feet.
Clouds in the heart remember the taste of the tears rolling down on her cheeks…

(Translator's note: *Norimaki* = Sushi role made with dried seaweed)

11

（俊/Shuntarō）

巨大な氷惑星と呼ばれている海王星の
表面温度は摂氏マイナス２１８度
中心温度は５０００度
体温３６度５分の私は地球上の室温２１度の部屋で
４月７日１２時１６分現在 生存中で〜す

거대한 얼음 행성으로 분류되는 해왕성
구름의 표면 온도는 섭씨 영하 218도
중심온도 5천도
지구 행성의 상온 21도에 방에 머무는 나의 체온은 36.5도,
4월 7일 12시 16분 지나 나는 아직 살아 있다(^^) !

海王星被称为"巨冰"行星
在云端，表面温度摄氏零下218
中心温度5000
而在地球上21度常温的房间里，我体温36.5
4月7日12点16分，还活着˜

The temperature of Neptune, categorized as 'ice giant', is
minus 218 degrees Celsius at its cloud tops, and
5,000 degrees at its center. I, with a body temperature of 36.5 degrees,
in a 21-degree room on planet Earth,
as of 16 minutes past 12 o'clock on the 7th of April, am still alive (^^)!

12

나는 책상 위에 해왕성에서 온 바다를 쏟는다
한 편의 시가 끝나자 우주 정거장의 불은 꺼졌다
나는 의자에 앉아 그 깜깜한 바닷물 속에 두 손을 담근다

海王星から海を掬って机の上に注ぐ
私たちの詩の最初の一巻が終わったら、宇宙の駅の灯りが消えた
私は椅子に座り両手を真っ黒な海原に浸す

我把海王星的海，泼在书桌上
我们的第一卷诗结束，灯光熄落在宇宙站台
我坐在椅子上，双手蘸进漆黑的海洋

I pour Neptune's sea on top of my desk
When our first round of poems is finished, the lights go out at the cosmos station
I sit in my chair and dip my hands into the pitch-black ocean

米の巻
米之卷
밥

THE ROLE OF 'RICE'

13

(迪/Mindy)

海水涌进稻田，一只海豚飞起
巨大的嘴，囤积稻米
它飞起，白色弥漫低矮的天空
它飞起，一个女人在奔跑——她要在太阳升起之前
把米藏好，留给那些孩子们

논에 쏟아진 파도처럼
거대한 입안에 쌀을 비축한 돌고래가 날아오른다
낮은 하늘을 하얗게 흩어놓으며—날아간다
해가 지기 전에 아이들 먹이려고 여자는 쌀을 숨겨 놓고 싶고——
바쁘게 달려가는 그 여자 위로—날아간다

海の波が水田に流れこむと、イルカが一匹飛び跳ねる、
大きな口のなかには米がぎっしり。
イルカは飛ぶ——空の底を白く滲ませて。
イルカは飛ぶ——女がひとり走ってゆく——米を隠したいのだ
子供たちのために、陽が昇らないうちに。

As the ocean spills into the rice fields, a dolphin flies up,
its huge mouth hoarding rice.
It flies—white diffuses the low sky.
It flies—a woman is on the run—she wants to hide the rice (米)
for the children before the sun rises.

ごはんつぶがひとつ、「父」
という漢字のあごひげのさきっぽにくっついている
まいごのちいさなかみさまみたいに

一粒煮熟的米饭悬挂在
汉字"父"亲的胡须尖
像一个小神仙走迷了路

밥알이 한자 아비 "父"
수염 끝에 매달려 있다
잃어버린 작은 신처럼

A grain of cooked rice is hanging
from the tip of the beard of Chinese character '父(father)',
like a little god who got lost.

15

（俊/Shuntarō）

一本脚の威厳を保っていた案山子は
鳥追いの役目を終えて
異郷の民族学博物館で余生を過ごしている
棚田と違ってそこには空がない
小学生が三人ガラスケースにへばりついている

왼 다리 하나로 존재의 위엄을 갖춘 허수아비가
까마귀 사냥꾼 역할을 마치고선
외국의 민족학 박물관에서 여생을 보내고 있다
다랭이논 같지 않은 그곳엔 하늘이 없다
세 명의 남학생 진열장에 얼굴을 눌러붙이고 있다

保持单腿尊严的稻草人
完成了赶乌鸦的任务
余生在异国一家民族学博物馆打发
与梯形稻田不同的是，那里没有天空
三个男生把脸贴在玻璃橱窗上看

The scarecrow who kept his dignity of being one-legged
finished his role as a crow chaser,
spending the rest of his life in a museum of ethnology in a foreign place.
He's got no sky, unlike on the terraced rice-fields.
Three schoolboys are pressing their faces to the glass showcase.

16

(惠/Hyesoon)

우리는 별의 혈육이듯 쌀의 혈육이다
흰 밥알을 삼켰을 뿐인데 어째서 빨간 피가 돌까?
밥을 먹지않는 곳으로 간 아이들이 별처럼 빛났다

私たちは米の血肉、星々の血と肉でもあるけれど
白米を一粒呑みこんだだけでも真紅の血が流れ巡るのはなぜだろう？
もう二度とご飯を食べられない場所へ旅立った子供たちは星のように瞬いている

我们是大米的血肉，如同星辰的血肉
我只吞下一粒白米饭，怎么就有深红的血液在流？
那些离开的孩子们，去了一个没有米的地方，像星星发出微光

We are the flesh and blood of rice, like the flesh and blood of the stars
How is it that crimson blood flows when I've only swallowed a single grain of white rice?
Children who've departed to a place where they won't be eating rice anymore shimmer like stars

17

大米稀缺。连天空都关闭了。
茨维塔耶娃又一次被拒。
她看上去比一只鸟还瘦，眼窝深陷……
我惊醒，看见头顶有九个月亮，
九个月神端着九碗白米饭，伸向快饿死的孤儿……

쌀이 동났다. 심지어 하늘이 닫혔다.
쯔베태바가 에게 곡기가 끊어졌다, 다시.
그녀는 새처럼 말랐다 그녀의 눈이 푹 꺼졌다……
나는 놀라서 일어났다 아홉 개 달이 내 머리 위에 떠 있고——
아홉 명의 여신이 아홉 개의 밥그릇을 그녀의 배 고픈 고아들 앞에 내밀었다……

米は尽きた。空までが閉じてしまった。
ツヴェターエワは拒絶された、またしても。
いまや鳥よりも痩せ細り、眼は落ち窪んで……
私ははっと目を覚ます、月が九個頭上に昇っているのが見える——
餓えて死にかけた彼女の孤児に九人の女神が九杯のご飯を差し出している……

Rice was scarce. Even the skies closed down.
Tsvetaeva was rejected, again.
She looked thinner than a bird, her eyes sunken...
I wake up startled, and see nine moons above me—
nine goddesses offering nine bowls of rice to her starved orphan...

18

若い僧の托鉢の椀に一握りの米
若葉が日の光に輝いている
崩れかかった土塀に沿って歩いてゆく

年轻的乞丐神父端着只有十几粒米的碗
阳光落在新鲜的叶子上
他走在摇摇欲坠的土墙上

어린 탁발승의 발우엔 밥이 가득하고
싱그러운 이파리들이 햇빛에 반짝인다
탁발승이 무너진 진흙벽을 따라 걸어가고 있다

A handful of rice in the bowl of a young mendicant priest.
Sunlight falls on fresh leaves.
He walks along a crumbling mud wall.

19

(康/Yasuhiro)

決して立ち止まるなと異国の師は僕に教えた
城壁を越え半島を抜け海峡を渡り
道は自らの歩みのなかにこそあるのだと
米粒に託された遠い甘さを噛みしめながら峠を降りると
懐かしい祭囃子の笛太鼓

가만히 서 있지 마라, 타국에서 스승이 말했다
요새들을 건너, 반도를 지나, 해협을 넘어
길은 걸어가는 행위에 의해 놓인다고 그는 말했다
쌀알이 가져다 준 오랜 단맛을 저작하면서, 길을 걸어 내려갔다
——친숙한 축제 밴드의 휘파람과 드럼 소리

不要站在原地——身处异国的师傅告诫我。
穿过城墙，走过半岛，越过海峡，
道路就在行走之中，他说。
我咀嚼着米粒带来的遥远甜味，沿着山路往下走
——熟悉的节日乐队，口哨声，鼓点声。

Never stand still, so my master taught me in a foreign land.
Across the fortress walls, through the peninsula, and over the straits,
the path lies in the very act of walking, he said.
Chewing the distant sweetness carried by grains of rice, I came down from the pass
—the familiar festival band of whistles and drums.

20

벚꽃 축제행렬이 지나간 뒤 나무 밑의 종이 사발이 흰 꽃을 먹고 있다
오랜만에 우리 식구 셋이 맨홀 뚜껑 같은 식탁 위에 그릇을 올려놓고 밥 먹는다
우리의 머리 위엔 하늘이 입을 벌리고, 우리의 발밑엔 하수구가 입을 벌리고 있다

花見のパレードが通り過ぎた後の桜の下で、紙皿が白い花びらを食べている
我が三人家族はもう久しくマンホールの蓋に似た食卓の上の椀から飯を食べていない
我らの頭上に空は口を開け、足元には下水が口を開いている

櫻花游行队伍走过之后，一个纸碗在树下吃白色的花瓣
我们一家三口已经很久没有在厨房餐桌上的砂锅里吃饭了
头上，天空开口，脚下，阴沟开口

After the cherry blossom parade has passed by, a paper bowl under the tree eats white petals
It's been a while since my family of three has eaten rice from bowls set on the manhole-cover-like
    kitchen table
Above our heads the sky opens its mouth, and beneath our feet the sewer opens its mouth

（俊/Shuntarō）

マナ　ヘブライ語で〈これは何だろう〉という名の食べ物
満腹した後にまだ飢えているのが人間だとしたら
その空腹は〈マナ〉という疑問のせいなのだ
たった一つのお握りが宝石だった敗戦後の少年には
魂の飢えよりも肉体の飢えのほうが切実だったが

玛纳，这种食物的名字，希伯来语"这是什么？"
如果人类满脑肥肠还感觉饥饿
饥饿由"这是什么"的问题引起
对这个男孩来说，战败后，一个饭团就是一颗珠宝
他发现身体饥饿比精神饥饿更真实

만나, 히브리어로 '이게 뭐야?' 라는 뜻을 가진 음식
인류가 포만감을 갖고서도 계속 배고픔을 느낀다면
배고픔이란 '만나'라고 불리는 질문에 의해 야기되는 것
비록 전후에 주먹밥을 보석보다 소중하게 여기는 소년이
영혼의 허기보다 육체의 허기를 더 실감했을지라도

Manna　　the food whose name means 'what is it?' in Hebrew.
If human beings are such that they feel hungry even with their stomachs full,
that hunger is caused by the question called 'Manna',
although the boy, for whom just one rice ball was worth a jewel after the defeat of the war,
found physical hunger more real than spiritual hunger.

(康/Yasuhiro)

ママは歴史の教科書を鵜呑みにしちゃだめよって言ったけれど
曾お祖父ちゃんの日記はどうなんだろう？
その次の数ページはご飯を煮て作った糊で閉じられている

엄마는 나에게 역사교과서를 맹목적으로 믿지 말라고 말했다,
그러나 내 증조할아버지의 일기는 어떤가?
밥알로 만든 풀로 나머지 몇 장이 봉해져 있다

母亲告诉我，别盲目相信历史教科书
那么我曾祖父的日记呢？
下面几页被米饭做的浆糊粘住

Mom told me not to blindly believe the history textbooks,
but what about my great grandfather's diary?
The next few pages are sealed with glue made of boiled rice.

23

（惠/Hyesoon）

내가 물을 마시면 물이 나를 마신다
내가 밥을 먹으면 밥이 나를 먹는다
내가 산소를 마시면 산소가 나를 먹는다
내가 먹으면 먹을수록 내 몸이 땅에 들러붙는다
감옥의 죄수가 밥알을 뭉개어 부처를 만든다

私が水を飲むと、水が私を飲む
私が米を食べると、米が私を食べる
私が酸素を吸い込むと、酸素が私を食べる
食べれば食べるほど私の体は地面に張り付いてゆく
独房の囚人は米を捏ねて仏陀を作る

我喝水的时候，水喝我
我吃饭的时候，饭吃我
我呼吸氧气，氧气吃我
我吃得越多，我的身体就越被粘在地上
一个囚犯在牢房里碾米，制作菩萨

When I drink water, the water drinks me
When I eat rice, the rice eats me
When I breathe in oxygen, the oxygen eats me
The more I eat the more my body is glued to the ground
The prisoner in a cell mashes rice to make Buddha

（迪/Mindy）

神农，五谷大帝，用眼中的阳光
给群山施肥，他种稻子，死于稻子，种草药，死于草药。
我奶奶埋葬他一千次，在他身体上种下一棵苹果树。

신농, 곡식의 신, 그의 눈에서 나온 햇빛이 산들을 비옥하게 하였다
그는 쌀을 심었고, 쌀로 죽었다, 약초를 심었고 약초로 죽었다
할머니는 천 번이나 그를 파묻었고 그의 몸 위에 사과 나무를 심었다

五穀の神である神農は、自分の眼から放つ日光で
山々を肥沃にした。米を植え米に死に、薬草を植え薬草に死んだ。
私の祖母は千回彼を埋葬し、その亡骸に一粒の林檎の種子を蒔いた。

Shennong, god of five grains, fertilized mountains with sunlight
from his eyes. He planted rice and died of rice, planted herbs and died of herbs.
My grandma buried him a thousand times and on his body planted an apple tree.

太陽の巻

日之卷

태양

THE ROLE OF 'SUN'

25

日本では国旗を日の丸と呼ぶ
白地に真紅の円だけのグッドデザイン
まるで子供が考えたかのような無邪気さだが
含意は五輪の五色どころではない色々
旗振りなど金輪際したくない

日本国旗叫日之丸（太阳盘）
所谓"好设计"，白底红圈
看上去那么无辜，像一个孩子的设想
但外观欺骗，它不吉利的多色不同于奥运会五彩环
而我永远不会摇这面旗帜

일본 국기는 히노마루 (태양의 원반) 라고 불린다
소위 '좋은 디자인' 흰 바탕에 새빨간 동그라미
아기가 생각해 낸 것처럼 순수한 모습
그러나 그것은 속임수, 그것은 오륜기의 다섯 색깔과는 다르게 불길한 색깔들의 배합이다
나는 그 깃발을 다시는 흔들지 않으리

The national flag of Japan is called Hinomaru (a sun disk).
A so-called 'Good Design' with just a crimson circle on the white background.
It looks so innocent that it might have been conceived of by a child,
but its appearance is deceiving: it's ominously multicolored, unlike the five colors of the Olympic rings.
I will never ever wave the flag.

（惠/Hyesoon）

쿠스코의 삭사이와만에서 태양의 축제가 있는 날이었다
나는 동지의 아침에서 하지의 서울의 밤에게 안녕 인사했다
365일 동안 계속될 마라톤 코스의 출발선에 인디오들이 가득했다

クスコのサクサイワマンにて、太陽の祭の日のこと
私は冬至の朝にハーイ！と呼びかけた夏至のソウルの夜に向かって
３６５日マラソンの出発ラインはインディオたちの熱気でむんむんしている

这天是库斯科的萨克塞萨瓦曼太阳节
我向首尔的夏至夜晚说一声冬至的早安
365天马拉松长跑的起跑线上站满了印度人

It was the day of the festival of the sun at Sacsayhuaman in Cuzco
I said hi in the morning of the winter solstice to Seoul's night in the summer solstice
The starting line of the 365-day long marathon was teeming with Indians

(康/Yasuhiro)

さまよえるペルー人たちの歌声が
ケーキ屋の店先のジングルベルと混じり合っている
男は全国新聞五紙を身体じゅうに巻きつけて
立ちはだかるビルの隙間に身を横たえる　彼は知っているのだ
そこが最初に<朝日>の射しこむ場所であることを

秘鲁流浪者的歌唱声
与糖果店前的叮当铃声，混合在一起。
一个流浪汉用五种全国性报纸裹住自己，
躺在一排建筑的圣圈里……他知道
清晨第一缕阳光（朝日）会照到那里。

방랑하는 페루 사람들의 노래 소리와
제과점 앞에서 흘러나오는 징글벨 소리가 서로 섞였다.
5개의 일간지로 몸을 감은 남자는
줄지어 선 빌딩들의 텅 빈 곳에 누워 있다......그는 알고 있다
그 곳에 아침 해의 첫 광선(아사히)이 닿으리라는 것을

The singing voices of the wandering Peruvians mix together
with Jingle Bells from the shop front of a confectioner's.
The man wraps himself in all 5 national newspapers
and lies down in the hollow of the lined-up buildings…he knows
that spot will get the first ray of the morning sun (Asahi).

28

（迪/Mindy）

一头拉美丛林的狮子站起，摇一头金色的头发。
洛尔迦在西班牙倒下，低头之前看见一个金色的太阳。
他抓住一根光线，仿佛牵住了一只古时候的和平风筝。

중남미 밀림의 금빛 갈기를 흔드는 사자가 있다
스페인에서 로르까는 총을 맞고 눈을 감기 전에 금빛 태양을 보았다
그는 고대의 평화로 나는 연줄을 꽉 잡은 것처럼 빛의 줄기를 꼭 잡았다

中南米の密林でライオンは金色の鬣を震わせている
スペインのロルカは眼を閉じる直前、金色の太陽を見ていた
彼は一筋の光を掴んでいたのだ古代の平和の凧の糸を掴もうとするかのように

There is a lion in Latin American jungles that swings its golden hair.
In Spain, Lorca saw a golden sun (日) before he closed his eyes.
He held a stream of light as if holding the string of an ancient peaceful kite.

29

（惠/Hyesoon）

올빼미는 저 빛이 얼마나 아플까?
동굴 속 박쥐는 저 빛이 얼마나 아플까?
다락방에 숨은 소녀는 저 빛이 얼마나 아플까?
밖에서는 불의 군대가 금빛 갈기를 앞세우고 행진해 오는데
새벽의 마지막 샛별을 움켜쥔 나는 얼마나 무서울까

光はどんなに痛いだろう梟にとって
光はどんなに痛いだろう洞窟のなかの蝙蝠にとって
光はどんなに痛いだろう屋根裏に隠れている少女にとって
外では、炎の軍隊が金色の鬣を振りかざして私の方へ行進してくる
私はどんなに怖がっていることだろう、朝空の最後の星にしがみついて

光，猫头鹰看见了一定是多么痛苦
光，洞穴里的蝙蝠看见了一定是多么痛苦
光，躲在阁楼里的小女孩看见了一定是多么痛苦
外面，火向我进军，带着一头金色的鬃毛
我一定是多么恐惧，拽着最后一颗晨星

How painful the light must be for the owl
How painful the light must be for the bat inside a cave
How painful the light must be for the girl hiding in the attic
Outside, the army of fire marches towards me with its golden mane
How frightened I must be, clutching onto the last morning star

(俊/Shuntarō)

ディスプレーに捉えられた虹がクリック一つで色を失う
「写真に色は要らない、光と影だけでいいの」と
銀髪のカメラウーマンは若い助手に向かってのたまう

一个点击，彩虹被显示屏捕捉，失色
"摄影不应该与颜色调情，光和影就足够"
银发女摄影师如是宣告，面向她的年轻助手

찰칵, 화면의 무지개가 색을 잃는다
"사진은 색을 갖고 놀지 말아야 한다, 사진은 빛과 그림자로 충분하다"
은발의 여성 사진작가가 그녀의 어린 조수에게 말한다

A click, and the rainbow caught on a display loses its color.
"Photography shouldn't flirt with color, just light and shadow is enough"
declares the silver-haired female photographer to her young assistant.

31

（迪/Mindy）

世界年轻时，女娲生下十个太阳
十个太阳十种颜色，十种性别
他们在空中玩耍，如同军阀，他们的狂热烧死了所有的飞鸟
一个女-男孩，手握一把弓，十支箭
把九个太阳射开，分割成九个海洋，九座火山……

이 세상이 아직 젊었을 때
여와는 열 가지 색과 열 가지 성을 가진 열 개의 태양을 낳았다
그들은 전쟁하는 장군들처럼 열광적으로 공중에서 날아다니는 새들을 태우면서 놀았다
소년/소녀가 활 하나와 화살 열 개를 들고 아홉 개의 태양을 쪼개자
아홉 개의 대양과 화산이 탄생했다

世界がまだ幼かった頃
女娲（じょか）は十の色と十の性を持つ十の太陽を産んだ
太陽たちは軍閥さながら空中で暴れまわり、飛ぶ鳥を悉く焼き尽くした
弓と十本の矢を手にした、男でも女でもあるひとりの子が、太陽のうち九つを砕いて
九つの海と九つの火山を作った……

When the world was still young
Nüwa gave birth to ten suns, of ten colors and ten genders.
They played around in the air like warlords and feverishly burnt all the flying birds.
A boy-girl, a bow and ten arrows in hand, split nine of the suns
into nine oceans and nine volcanic mountains…

32

日時計盤の上を蟻が這ってゆく
昼から夜へと　蝶の翅を引きずりながら
地底の子等へのご馳走に

一只蚂蚁在日晷上爬行
从早到晚，拖着一只蝴蝶的翅膀
给地底下的小伙伴们带来一顿盛宴

개미 한 마리가 해시계를 넘어간다
종일토록 나비의 날개를 끌고 간다
땅 속의 새끼를 먹이려고

An ant is crawling on a sundial
from day to night, dragging the wing of a butterfly.
A treat for the little ones underground.

33

（惠/Hyesoon）

수화 교실에선 소리 대신 빛으로 종을 친다
수업이 끝나는 시간도 점심시간도 빛으로 종을 친다
축구의 파울은 심판이 뛰어와서 친절하게 알려 준다
손목시계를 들여다보던 심판이 게임의 종료 깃발을 높이 들어 올리면
이긴 팀도 진 팀도, 심판도 관중도 두 손으로 나비를 만들어 햇빛 속에 날린다

手話を教える教室ではベルの代わりに光が鳴る
光は授業の終わりに鳴り昼休みにも鳴る
サッカーの審判が駆け寄って礼儀正しく反則の判定を下す
手元の時計を見つめていた審判が高々と旗を掲げて試合終了を告げると
勝ったチームも負けた方も、審判も観衆も、両手で蝶を作って陽光の中へ解き放つ

在手语教室里，一束光代替了一阵铃声
光在课后和午餐时鸣响
一个足球裁判跑过去，礼貌地判了一次违规
裁判盯着手表，比赛结束，举起旗子
输赢双方，裁判与观众，都打出蝴蝶手势，然后对着阳光松开手

In the sign language classroom a light rings instead of a bell
The light rings at the end of class and also at lunch
A soccer referee runs over and politely makes a foul call
When the referee who was staring at his watch raises the flag at the end of the game
the winning and losing teams, the referee and spectators make butterflies with theirs hands and
    release them into the sunlight

(康/Yasuhiro)

窓ガラス越しに見下ろすとどんな風景も詩的に見える
と演説の原稿を仕上げながら独裁者は思う
彼を憎む人々の海の波間に眼鏡のレンズがきらきら瞬いている

从玻璃窗往下看到的景致似乎都有诗意
反照着暴君，他正给讲演稿最后点缀几笔
痛恨他的人海波涛上，眼镜片在闪光

창문 유리를 통해 내려다 보이는 어떤 풍경도 시적이다,
연설 원고의 마지막 손질을 하는 독재자가 생각한다
그를 싫어하는 군중의 파도위에, 그들의 안경 렌즈들이 반짝인다

Any scene when viewed through the window pane looks poetic,
reflects the tyrant as he gives the finishing touch to his speech.
On the waves of the sea of people who hate him, the lenses of their glasses glitter.

35

（迪／Mindy）

我叔叔戴着单片眼镜追一只中国坛子，
我戴两片黄瓜追他。从两个被虫咬开的洞
我看见一朵太阳花引路，把我引到长江边——
屈原曾从这里跳下去，我给他带来两千个粽子。
他站起来目光炯炯，左眼金星，右眼荷花。

외알 안경을 쓴 내 삼촌은 중국 단지를 쫓고
나는 오이조각 두개를 눈에 붙이고 그를 쫓는다. 벌레가 씹어놓은 좁은 구멍으로
나는 해바라기가 이끄는 길을 바라보고 그 길은 나를 양쯔강으로 데려간다
굴원은 이곳에서 강으로 뛰어내렸다……나는 그에게 쌀로 만든 쫑쯔를 던져주었다
그가 일어서자, 눈빛이 형형했다, 그의 왼쪽 눈은 금성, 오른쪽 눈은 연꽃

片眼鏡をかけて、私の叔父さんは中国の瓶を追いかける。
私は二枚のキュウリの薄切りをつけて叔父さんの後を追う。虫食いの小さな穴から
ヒマワリが私を導いて揚子江に連れて行くのが見える——
屈原はここから飛び込んだのだ……私は彼にちまきを用意してきた。
彼は眼光爛々と立ち上がる、その左眼は金星、右目は蓮の花と化している。

With his monocle, my uncle chases a Chinese jar.
I put on two slices of cucumber to chase after him. Through the pin holes of insect bites
I see a sunflower that leads the way, bringing me to the Yangtze River instead—
Qu Yuan had jumped from here… I've brought bamboo leaves filled with sticky rice.
He stands up, beaming, his left eye Venus, his right eye a lotus.

47

36

（俊/Shuntarō)

時代の風にあおられ古代の光に灼かれながらも
私たちの曼荼羅は詩で世界のエントロピーに抗う
こっちの夕日はそっちの朝日　お休みとお早うは螺旋状に明日へと向かう

本世纪的风吹过，古时候的光烧过
曼陀罗仍旧以诗抗拒世界的无序
此夕阳是彼朝阳，晚安和晨安向明天螺旋移动

시대의 바람으로 날리고 고대의 빛으로 태워진
시로써 세상의 엔트로피에 아직도 저항하는 우리의 만달라.
여기의 저녁 해는 저기의 아침 해. 잘 자요, 좋은 아침 내일을 향해 소용돌이로 움직여간다

Blown by the winds of the era and burned by the ancient lights,
our mandala still resists with poetry against the world's entropy.
The evening sun here is the morning sun over there   Good night and good morning move towards
    tomorrow in a spiral.

TRILINGUAL RENSHI CHRONICLE

March 5, 2015 Listening to the BBC World News about ISIS at home in Munich, my mind drifts to the news from Japan. Our Prime Minister would make a World War II 70th anniversary speech in August and has appointed a committee for its preparation. I find it both dismaying and ludicrous. Committee to advise on what to be said and what not? Linguistic examination on the political connotation of "Remorse" or "Repentance"? How can you expect an honest and sincere speech that way? And why bother with the words, anyway? Politician should be a man of action rather than of word. Leave the matter of rhetoric to poets… The next moment, I am being struck with this crazy idea: what if I organize a Renshi session with poets from China and Korea and publish the result on August 15, just as Prime Minister delivers his speech? Or better yet, how about reading it together on one of those disputed islands…?

March 6 I share my idea with Mindy, whose poems I translated into Japanese recently. Looking back, perhaps the e-mail conversation I had with her in the process of the translation was at the back of my mind in the previous evening. To my question about her national identity, which I often ask to myself, she wrote back, *"there is so much to feel in life that I don't really pay attention to 'Citizenship' which is a stupid word or stupid thing…"*

March 7 Mindy writes back from across the ocean, *"Great idea. I would love to join you."* All of a sudden, it doesn't sound crazy anymore. I then write to Michael Brennan, an Australian poet who is publishing poets in Asia and Oceania from his own publishing house, and Mia You, who was born in Korea and is central editor of Poetry International Rotterdam, in search for Korean poets.

March 14 Not only do Michael and Mia You introduce to me several Korean poets, they also express strong support for the idea. I follow one of their leads and reach Don Mee Choi, a poet and translator born in Seoul and grew up in the US, and then Kim Hyesoon, whose poems Don Mee has translated into English.

March 16 Don Mee writes, *"Kim Hyesoon says she would like to participate…I'm very glad about her decision! I will take full responsibility of translating her poems."* At this moment, the crazy idea becomes a reality…well, almost.

March 21 Mindy, Don Mee and I have been wondering whether we should do this with 3 poets, or 6 poets (a couple each from 3 countries). In case of 6, Don Mee and Kim Hyesoon would team up. I ask Shuntarō Tanikawa about his interest and Mindy explores her contacts in China. We like the idea of 6 because of the diversity, but we worry about the extra time required for translation and coordination. Can we finish everything by August 15? After consulting with her calendar during the summer time, Don Mee decides that she should rather concentrate on translating Kim Hyesoon this time. But then Shuntarō comes back saying, *"I'm interested in it"* and I just cannot resist the temptation of writing together with him (I did a couple of sessions with him before and, boy, what a rewarding experience it was!).

March 24   I argue to the team that, while it may be politically correct to keep the balance among the three countries, Shun should really not count as Japanese poet. Because of his cosmic vision and extraterrestrial sensitivity, as the title of his debut book *Alone in Two Billion Light Years* indicates, he was often called as "Space Man". So he represents the universe in this session! The team, apparently out of pity, accepts my plea and we reach our conclusion: 4 poets, 9 rounds, 36 linked poems. We shall follow the 5 and 3 lines convention, which was developed through the numerous Renshi sessions by a group of Japanese poets including Makoto Ooka and Shuntarō back in 1960's and 70's. If I did not meet the two poets in my 20's, I would never be doing this right now. I also propose to set a general theme for each of the 3 rounds and suggest "Sea" for the first 3 rounds. Maybe "Rice" for the second 3 rounds, something we have in common…

March 28   I write the first 5 lines, *Hokku* or the opening poem, and send to the team, as I pack my suitcase for traveling to Japan over the next two weeks. My thinking goes: *if I sent it right before my departure, it will probably take 2 weeks to complete the first round, so I can relax during my stay in Japan…*

I was wrong. By the time I got to Munich Airport for departure on April 1, Shuntarō already sent to me his poem No.4, completing the first round. When I left Haneda Aiport 14 days later, we were halfway through at poem No.15. Almost every morning, I found a new poem waiting for me in my laptop. It seemed that the poets, me included, simply could not help but write their 5 or 3 lines as soon as they got the preceding poem. At one point, Mindy even sent her poem even though it was not her turn yet. And there was another trick: the time difference between the US West Coast where Mindy and Don Mee live and Korea / Japan. When one side was in bed sleeping, the other side was up and writing. It was a 24 hour non-stop global production!

I wrote my poem No.10 as I was actually flying over the Suruga Bay and looking down at Mt. Fuji, although "norimaki" is a fictional device to link with Mindy's poem No.9 via 'seaweed'. "A grain of rice" in No.14 was in fact hanging from the beard of my father, whom I visited in Kyushu and had dinner with. It was a dreamlike experience of living in two worlds at the same time: one in reality and the other in language, the two intertwining with each other. When I received Mindy's poem No.13 about a dolphin flying up from the flooded rice field, I thought it might be from an ancient Chinese legend and googled it up. As it turned out, it was purely Mindy's imagination but guess what I found in the google search? A news report about a dolphin trapped in an inland rice field after the 3.11 tsunami!

The teaching of "never stand still", just keep going forward, in my poem No.19 is essentially what I had learned from Makoto Ooka as the most basic rule of Renshi. But there was one moment when we stood still, not knowing how to move on. That was when Shuntarō wrote his poem No.25 about Hinomaru Japanese flag. To me, it was a baldly personal, courageous statement against nationalism. I translated it into English and sent to Don Mee with a short comment *"Wow!"* Don Mee replied *"Wow, indeed!"* But Hyesoon expressed her concern that readers in her country may misunderstand the poem as a praise for the flag and its historical association. I passed her remark to Shuntarō, who happened to be in Seoul that day for another poetry event! He understood Hyesoon's concern and offered to modify the text. Hyesoon could not visit Shuntarō in his Seoul event but the two poets found a mutual acquaintance, Shuntarō's editor and Hyesoon's former student. In the meanwhile, I realized that the problem, at least partly, stemmed from my English translation which was rather vague and open to interpretation, especially the first 4 lines. Don Mee and I worked together on the revised translation. I also shared the whole situation with Mindy, who wrote back, *"I think I understand Shuntarō. As poets we want to be non-political but maintain the basic humanistic principle."* Then, on April 23, came Hyesoon's message via Don Mee, *"Kim Hyesoon says she is so thankful for your explanation of Shuntarō's intention and for the revision (of the English translation) text). Now it is clear to her. She wanted me to relay her deep gratitude to you!"*

That was a pivotal moment in our Renshi session. It somehow gave the collaboration among us a new dimension, and a new driving force. We were now closer to each other and able to feel the real persons behind the poems. And poems gushed out. We knew there was no need to hurry, we should rather take time and cherish this exhilarating experience, but to no avail. It was non-stoppable. And…

April 30   32 days after I sent my *Hokku*, I receive from Shuntarō his *Ageku*, the closing poem, No.36. I translate it in English and send it to the whole team including Michael and Mia. The session is over. Alone in Munich with no one around to give a toast with, I just sit still and look at the PC display. I realize then that we made not only the crazy idea come true but also the longest e-mail chain in my life with 98 messages linked together in a string.

Yasuhiro Yotsumoto
May 9, 2015 Munich

A TRAVELING POEM

This is a poem that travels across four countries, between four poets, and gets completed in four languages.

I met Yasuhiro Yotsumoto at the PI web editors' meeting in Rotterdam in 2013 and again at Cordoba festival in Spain in 2014. It's amazing that he is a poet from Wharton, the top B-school in the US (that's another story). In March of this year, he said to me, from Munich, Germany, that he would like to run a trilingual Renshi as a poetic counter-action on the anniversary of the ending of the World War II. I was in Vermont Studio Center/USA, across the Atlantic Ocean from him. It was snowing but I was lighted by his idea. By the time the chained-poetry started, I was back in the sunny California and he, after throwing the opening poem to us, flew to Japan, across the Pacific Ocean from me. Poetry circled in the air. As facilitator or moderator he reminded us to push the Renshi forward, forward, and forward.

It wasn't a marathon that I expected and was a little worried about. 36 poems were completed in about a month. 36 x 4 languages. Yasuhiro and I self-translated our poems into English, he also translated Shuntarō's poems, I translated them into Chinese, so on and so forth. Without the trips between the poems, we would have finished it even sooner. The whole month of April was email, email, email, from four directions. Yotsumoto means "four dollars" in Chinese, and in the old days Chinese dollars used to have a square in the middle with four corners. The fourth month of the year brought four moons above me each night, it was really crazy that I was doing four things at the same time: writing my own sequences (titled "Four Moons"), doing this 4p Renshi, translating Duo Duo from China, and collaborating with two young poets from San Diego in transforming Chinese visual poems into English. Renshi ended so quickly that I now miss Hyesoon's deep agony and passion from Korea (through Donmee Choi's beautiful translation), Shuntarō's humor from Japan and Yasuhiro's constantly changing personas.

The hardest part of doing this was moving "forward". A Renshi is a poem of poems created by different authors, one after another, linked together. You are part of it. You daydream you wrote everything. But you are only bits of it. Each one writes in his or her native language and you are so attempted to respond to everything but you have limited space and you have to move on. I always wanted to go back to Yasuhiro's initial poem to explore what's inside those suitcases and I had to imagine Piazza San Marco as other part of the world and other body of water and move on and on until I reached my homeland China and my home by the Yangtze River where Qu Yuan jumped in for all of us poets two thousand years ago and because I was physically in America I let Stevens play my "uncle" chasing the jar that my "great grandpa" Qu Yuan used to drink wine from but was somehow moved to Tennessee by some sort of guy like Pound. I'm not sure what I was doing in this Renshi. I was rambling around, picking up a grain from the previous poem and throwing a tamale to the next person, sometimes completely confused about the order. I traveled "forward" to the ancient time, "forward" to the outer space, and "forward" to my left atrium.

Ming Di
May 10, 2015 from California

P.S. Japanese poetry was introduced to China in 1916 but soon overshadowed by the influence of the Western Modernism. It's a great pity that we didn't learn enough from Japan. Ezra Pound learned from Haiku and became a better poet. China had 联句 (linking poetry) since Han dynasty, and Tang poets made it very popular, but since the New Cultural Movement in 1919 promoted "Overall Westernization" and "Down with the Old Traditions" we lost many interesting things including the fun of developing a possible new form of linking poetry. The most fascinating feature of Japanese poetry, to me, is 错落有致— irregularity in a patterned form, or freedom in a controlled way—from its ancient 5-7-5-7-7 metrical pattern to the contemporary free verse of 5-3-5-3 stanzas. Too bad that I forgot all about Haiku while doing this Renshi. 3-line always made me depressed while 5-line was always a paradise as I could put almost all the garbage in it. What I found most difficult was translating condensed lines. In No.6, "Republic" was a verb in Chinese: sailing to a sun that can "republicize" each of us. I was taking the deconstructive meanings of the compound word 共和 in Chinese: sharing the sun in harmony as individuals not as countries. I translated it as "Sun Republic" knowing that something got lost. But I enjoyed translating others into Chinese. I will tell Comrade Li Bai that it's been so much fun to write and translate at the same time.

POET BE GONE

Renshi is an unfamiliar genre in Korea. When I first encountered our Renshi project, I thought its rules might be too cumbersome like the rules of poetry enjoyed by the upper class men during the Chosun era, which involved several men taking turns to compose a line. I became anxious that my ability to breathe and float with the rhythm of the poem would be oppressed. As a Korean poet I have had previous traumas, which makes me overly sensitive to the slightest hint of constraint dictated from the outside. Our first theme was "sea."

Strangely, the same scene kept appearing in my mind, the scene of young students boarding a ferry. The scene appears along with the kind of communal excitement that takes hold of me when I am about to begin an orientation with my new students; the sweet and sickly scents that the young bodies exude from the excitement. The overwhelming scents move in from somewhere and the scene emerges. The poet is a citizen of afterimages. The place where the end begins again is the poet's space. At such a juncture, a soul remains forever in the moment of fleetingness after everyone has left the scene, and the poet even sets up home for the soul. The point where the end begins again, there is no "I" of the afterimage. The "I" exists as a lump, a bundle of experiences. One of the characteristics of afterimages is that they revisit the fleeting moment endlessly. They return. The verb that permits and drags along the motion of perception triggered at the moment of each return is all that the poet, the citizen of afterimages, possesses. The world of images keeps coming back even if all of you have forgotten or departed. The poet relives the scene endlessly as if digging a grave. The poet perpetually attains presentification, allowing the day, the moment to soar from the grave of language. The poet believes everything must be symbolized. As I began working on Renshi, I reminded myself of the small fringes of my afterimages. But as soon as I submitted my first poem, it felt as if the energy of my poem extended to the poets of China and Japan was severed because of my dark poem about the children boarding a ferry. But Yasuhiro, Shuntarō, and Mindy understood right away and let me know through e-mails that they were well aware of the Korean ferry tragedy.

I continued to recall the particles of afterimages. I thought about the motion of particles that moved from one matter to another, that extended from one person to another. I thought about the fluidity of the particles that had no borders. I thought about the fog that moved in outside the window at night while I stayed restless after turning off the live coverage of the capsizing of the ferry, which unfolded like a mirror. I thought about the particles that embraced my entire room like fog. I thought about the explosion of every single particle. But the particles whirled and sank endlessly. Like a mirror turned on all the time, the live TV coverage of the sinking was shown on the walls of my room. Whenever I tried to set the scene of the sinking ferry onto the world of language, the countless streams of anger, shame, and sorrow flowed backward, engulfing me. As the Renshi progressed, the sea or sea of letters that extended beyond the width of its skirt into the five seas and six continents capsized once it entered Korea's sea. Yasuhiro suggested, "Generally speaking, it is not recommended to repeat the same topic or image again and again in Renshi." This made me think about what I experienced after the tragedy, that the sea for a Korean poet was no longer a metaphor. Korean poets have lost the storehouse of metaphors called "sea." Language solidified and the mystery of poetry hardened. Language scooped up its own shadow from its interior. I could no longer write poetry.

The poet is now deprived of metaphors.
The sea is no longer the locus of metaphors.
XX said metaphorically in the poem: Going under water.
The vast world is tied with ribbons of metaphors.
I must ask for forgiveness.
The poet is now robbed of seasons.
Summer doesn't come after spring. A warm winter follows.
Flowers bloom all at once then die.
The flowers bud like the fists XX clenched in the poem.
I must ask for forgiveness for speaking metaphorically.

XX is now robbed of God.
It is now difficult to pray to God.

The above is not (part of) a poem. The line breaks don't make it a poem. It is a description or an essay. It is like a mask worn on a face dripping with sweat and tears. From that day of the tragedy, it was pitch dark even at daylight. Darkness fell on me. Pencils returned to their graphite state, ink spilled onto the ground. It was impossible to write poetry in the room of pitch-dark shame. Like language that has become useless to parents who have lost their children, poetry has also become useless. Isn't there a saying that poetry creates a world of usefulness with useless language? However, poetry has extinguished the fire inside the poet. The foundation, "us," is destroyed. In my destroyed state, I could not endure the shame of having taken part in the destruction. The poet was enwrapped in the manifestation of the parents who devour their own children in myths. I became locked up in the prison of shame. How is it that my country keeps stirring up the anguish and tragedy of the survivors day after day, year after year? The column I was writing for a literary journal came to a halt; my writing lost its voice. But I kept going to work in City of Ansan without fail. The citizens of Ansan wore black for an entire year, so I, too, commuted to and from work in black. Last spring, flowers were in bloom all at once as if caught in a shameful act, but no one talked about it. The petals blew in the wind along the streets of the city, its soul extinguished. I asked my students to write essays in place of an exam. Not one of them mentioned the sea in which the ferry capsized. Instead, they went to volunteer at the memorial site for those who perished in the sea. One student asked me: Are you able to write poetry at such a time as this? No, I couldn't at all. The "I," the poetic subject constructed by language, which propels the world of language and drives the present names to their death every second, was released. Only thing that was clear to me was the dichotomous world made up of intense pain on one end and language on the other. Language and pain pushed each other out. However, I still could not write.

XX dressed all in black goes to the city.
As the train gets near its destination, an announcement is made:
"If you are taking a shuttle bus to the memorial site, please get off at the next station."
"If you are walking, please get off at the station after the next one."
For heaven's sake, what kind of country has an announcement on the train about a funeral?

When my class is over, I go pay my last respect to the dead.
At the end of a long line, I lower my head and offer a bouquet of chrysanthemums.
As the line becomes shorter the fresh, clear, unblemished, and lively faces of the children who died weigh heavily on my mind.

The mourners are silent. They have come from afar.
No one complains despite the long wait.
They all cry after paying their last respects, offering chrysanthemums.
They are given several sheets of tissue as they leave.
Outside each mourner writes a letter.
To the place of endless darkness.
To the place of endless coldness.
To the place of endless bleakness.

They write, Hope to meet you again in another country.
Rest in peace in another country.

How easy it is to kill God,
XX thinks in the morning of Easter.

Everyone in this city goes about in black.
Nobody smiles.
The spring blossoms are noticeably vulgar.
XX despises the flowers in full bloom.
XX despises the pink blossoms.

The above is also not (part of) a poem. It is a diary. A surface. A record of facts with feelings attached to them. It is denotative. The inexpressible cannot be activated in the denotative world. Language that keeps running with a tail of nostalgia attached to its end has dried up, leaving behind an information-ridden language. In such language, there is no Lao Tzu's "valley", "darkness", or "woman" that are like the void, uterus, or hole where poetry can be alive again. In such language, there is no space for things and essence that shed their attire of being, no space for them to be nameless and live together, without borders, in disappearance; there is no space for poetry to live. One aspect of poetry is the poet's absence, the poet's symbolic death; poetry erodes the center through the poet's bareness and scarcity. By residing in the absence within her, by pitting her own death against poetry's death, she can cut across the center. Poetry, as it gasps, barely breathing, draws up absence, death from the world of overflowing practicality. The gaping hole in the middle of poetry, the placeless place, is the space of poetry. Poetry is filled with words, yet it embodies absence like the wheel's axis. Poetry is another reality captured through absence. The poet announces the reality's fast-approaching death with silence-filled words, and by doing so, meets her own death inside poetry. The poet is a being that lives because of death. A being that is neither dead nor alive. That is why those above sentences with line breaks are not (part of) a poem. In those shifting lines, the poet's presence is excessive. There is too much of the "I." I say only the words that I can. Poetry is a space where the inexpressible is expressed, but I fill it up by saying only the things that I can. The "I" dies in order to become the "I" in poetry, but in those sentences, I do not die. Since I have failed to die (noun), I am unable to express the world of experience with verbs only. Therefore, those lines are not a poem.

After the Sewol tragedy, I was unable to discard myself. The poet was not able to become the other. Can anyone imagine the hours the parents who have lost their children are left with? I thought about the despair of the parents who are not even able to safeguard their mourning and sorrow. I watched them endure the unavoidable pain of seeing their grief being subjected to generalization. The poet's space that should be full of absence and emptiness filled up with dark bile instead. After a whole year, not a thing has been made clear. How is this possible? They make our blood boil. Not a single individual has admitted responsibility. Which part of the leviathan, fattened by the web of neo-liberalism made of transparent reinforced steel, am I clinging to? Have I lived all these years unaware of the fact that I am caught in the web of perpetration? The questions and answers were exactly the same, adding to my despair. The poet's "valley," "darkness," "woman" were locked up, unable to conjure up even the poet's ghost. The poet was totally incapable of writing. I could not fall into the hole that floats around the realm of poetry inside me. I could not hear what my hole was saying. I tried hard to avoid the fact that my hole was connected to other holes like the sewers beneath the manhole cover. I was unable to relinquish myself. Like someone who suffers from pain might feel that she is an outcast, I also felt like an outcast in the world of poetry. I kept rejecting myself: Poet be gone. My valley was dead, turned into blackness. The poet's language is neither personal nor communal; it is suspended in between, on the cliffs of the boundaries. Then the words of poetry have no choice but to slip out from the gap between the inside and the outside. The poet is always under the dire predicament of having her life overlapped with the life outside her. But after the tragedy, I was too "alive" inside. I was filled with anger and sorrow instead of emptiness that is needed for poetry to emerge. I could not empty myself. I could not distance myself as the other. I could not activate my non-being. So I was unable to call out the name of the secret. I was unable to call out the experiences that are entangled with the secret's name.

As soon as the theme "sea" came to an end, "rice" and "sun" followed. Shuntarō began the theme of "sun" with the image of the flag of Japan and declared: "It looks so innocent that it might have been conceived of by a child… I will never ever wave the flag." These lines contained a kind of courage, which I could not express in words. I felt afraid that if I made a comment about it, I would only weaken the strength of the courage present in Shuntarō's words. The trilingual Renshi project allowed me to knock on the world of afterimages again. I was still afraid of opening the door, but once I accepted the invitation to take part in the project, my submerged face began to open the door; I started to feel as if I might have something to say. At the exhibition called *Children's Room,* held at the corner of a small shopping mall near the houses where the children once lived, I peered into the empty rooms of the children who perished in the sea. Their school uniforms, blankets and pillows, baseball gloves, bicycles, desks, reference books, and hangers. The pictures of their idols. Their future at a standstill. But most of all, the children's faces left in the middle of the empty playground after they had drifted away. I stayed silent and listened to the voices of the afterimages. The world left bare by all the emptiness was inside and outside me. I felt that the outside world of experience wanted to be embraced once again. That empty world where you and I are not divided, the calm, silent world, like the eye of a storm. I went out to that space and sensed the endless opening of the "valley," "darkness," "woman," and the rhythm of the breathing of a certain collective existence, collective emotion. The children's silence is in that space. The children's cries are the poet's death, their cries reborn through death into the kingdom of absence. The sound of the silence can only be detected when the "I," the poetic subject, dies. The cries of the silence prevent "I" who is filled with the closed "I" from encountering the name "I." The children can never be destroyed. Cherishing the children who had barely lived. The future of cherishing. The children are already born inside the infinite space the poet must enter. They appear in the infinite form of the smallest, the weakest, the banished.

Kim Hyesoon
May 2015, Seoul
(Translated by Park Ilhyung and Don Mee Choi)

THE THRILL AND JOY OF "TSUKEAI"

In the practice of traditional Renku, from which the modern Renshi originated, "Tsukeai" or the art of linking between verses is of critical importance. For Renshi, too, "Tsukeai" remains to be the challenge. How should you link your poem to the preceding one? If you link only in an explicit, denotational sense, it would result in a so-called "Betazuke" (sticky link), in which the time and space between the poems, something equivalent to "between-the-lines" of a text, become flat and prosaic. On the other hand, if you depend too much on connotation, you end up with the link which is self-centered and not understandable to others. Let me examine a few links of my own as examples.

Poem No.3 by Kim Hyesoon is overshadowed by the sinking of Sewol like a nightmare which repeats again and again. My poem No.4 is an attempt to link to it in a broader context. The modern ferry boat is transformed here into an ark in the age of mythology through the implication of the word "ship", generating in the process a sort of nihilistic twists such as "preceding life" and "out of the planet".

Yasuhiro Yotsumoto, when he wrote poem No.10, might be expecting me to expand his last line to a romance as in the traditional Japanese love songs, but I deliberately avoided that. Instead, I introduced the planet Neptune, which is regarded as the sea god, using dry and technical terms. With the "～" sign in the last line, which signals for the retreated state of mind of the narrator in today's Japanese writing system (but probably untranslatable), I tried to stay away from what is called "Mukouzuke" (link with contrasting characters or objects) in the traditional Renku.

In Renku, the last closing verse is called "Ageku" and supposed to be open-ended in happy celebration. Instead of being a specific response to Mindy's poem No.35, my Ageku No.36 is a self-reference to the entire process of our Renshi session, in a sense summarizing it. Following the spirit of "greeting" in Hokku (the opening verse) in the traditional Renku, I too gave my "greeting" in my last poem as the Ageku of this Renshi.

Shuntarō Tanikawa
May 7, 2015, Tokyo

ABOUT THE AUTHORS

Yasuhiro Yotsumoto, born in 1959 in Osaka, has published 10 poetry collections, one novel, and several books of translation and criticism in Japanese, and English translation of poetry *Family Room* (Vagabond Press, 2010). Yasuhiro's first experience of Renshi was *Shizuoka Renshi* in 2003 with Makoto Ooka, Masayo Koike, J. Bernlef, and Willem van Toorn. He also held two sessions with Shuntarō Tanikawa, Hiromi Ito, Wakako Kaku and Jerome Rothenberg in Kumamoto in 2008 and 2010, and another Shizuoka session with Kiwao Nomura, Wakako Kaku, Aki Ooka, and Tian Yuan in 2010. In the one-on-one Taishi (対詩) format, Yasuhiro collaborated with Masayo Koike (『詩と生活』 *Life vs Poetry*, Shichosha, 2005) and with Inuo Taguchi (『泥の暦』 *Muddy Calendar*, Shichosha, 2008). Based in Munich, Germany, where he has lived for 21 years, Yasuhiro serves as editor for a Japanese poetry magazine 'Beagle' and for Poetry International Rotterdam.

Ming Di 明迪 (aka Mindy), born in China, is a poet and translator, author of six books of poetry in Chinese. Some of her poems have been translated into other languages: *River Merchant's Wife* (Marick Press/USA, 2012), *Luna fracturada* (Valparaíso/Spain, 2014), *Histoire de famille* (Transignum/France, 2015) and *Livre de sept vies* (forthcoming in France). She has translated four books of poetry/poetry criticism into Chinese and co-translated four volumes of poetry from Chinese into English including *The Book of Cranes* (Vagabond Press 2015) and *Empty Chairs* (Graywolf Press 2015). She edited and co-translated *New Cathay: Contemporary Chinese Poetry* (Tupelo Press, co-published by the Poetry Foundation, 2013). She went to Boston College and Boston University for graduate study in linguistics, taught Chinese at BU before settling in California. At present she divides her time between California and Beijing.

Kim Hyesoon, one of the most prominent Korean poets, was born in 1955, South Korea. She debuted in 1979 and has ten collections of poetry published by Munji: *From Another Star* (1981), *Father's Scarecrow* (1984), *The Hell of a Certain Star* (1987), *Our Negative Picture* (1991), *My Upanishad, Seoul* (1994), *Poor Love Machine* (1997), *To the Calendar Factory Supervisor* (2000), *A Glass of Red Mirror* (2004), *Your First* (2008), and *Sorrowtoothpaste, Mirrorcream* (2011). Her poetry in translation include: *When the Plug Gets Unplugged* (Tinfish, 2005), *Anxiety of Words: Contemporary Poetry by Korean Women* (Zephyr, 2006), *Mommy Must Be a Fountain of Feathers* (Action Books, 2008), *All the Garbage of the World, Unite!* (Action Books, 2011), *Sorrowtoothpaste Mirrorcream* (Action Books, 2014), and *I'm OK, I'm Pig* (Bloodaxe Books, 2014). This is her very first participation in writing of Renshi.

Shuntarō Tanikawa was born in 1931 in Tokyo. The most widely read and critically important poet in today's Japan, Tanikawa is one of the pioneers who have brought the traditional Renku (連句) back to the modern practice as Renshi (連詩). Together with the members of poetry group *Kai* (Oar), he published *Kai Renshi* in 1979. Tanikawa's Renshi collaborations soon went beyond Japan to the foreign poets, as can be seen in *Vier Scharniere Mit Zunge*, with H.C. Artmann, Oscar Pastior, and Makoto Ooka (Berlin: Verlag Klaus G. Renner, 1988). His recent activities in this area include one-on-one Renshi, or Taishi (対詩), with Swiss poet Jürg Halter (*Sprechendes Wasser*, Bern: Sessions, 2012), and another Taishi with Korean poet Shin Kyeong-nim (*Take time to enjoy Makgeolli because we don't drink it just to get drunk*, Tokyo: CUON, 2015) .

Don Mee Choi (Translator of Kim's Renshi) is the author of *The Morning News Is Exciting* (Action Books, 2010), and translator of contemporary Korean women poets. She has received a Whiting Writers Award and the 2012 Lucien Stryk Translation Prize. Her translation of Kim Hyesoon's *Sorrowtoothpaste Mirrorcream* (Action Books, 2014) was shortlisted for the 2015 PEN Poetry in Translation Award. Her most recent works include a chapbook, *Petite Manifesto* (Vagabond Press, 2014), and a pamphlet, *Freely Frayed, ㅋ=q, Race=Nation* (Wave Books, 2014). Her second book of poems, *Hardly War*, is forthcoming from Wave Books in April 2016.

www.ingramcontent.com/pod-product-compliance
Lightning Source LLC
Chambersburg PA
CBHW061407090426
42739CB00021B/3497